D1714831

Cultural Celebrations

CHRISTMAS

DiscoverRoo
An Imprint of Pop!
popbooksonline.com

Rachel Hamby

abdobooks.com

Published by Pop!, a division of ABDO, PO Box 398166, Minneapolis, Minnesota 55439. Copyright © 2021 by POP, LLC. International copyrights reserved in all countries. No part of this book may be reproduced in any form without written permission from the publisher. Pop!™ is a trademark and logo of POP, LLC.

Printed in the United States of America, North Mankato, Minnesota.

052020
092020

♻ THIS BOOK CONTAINS RECYCLED MATERIALS

Cover Photo: Shutterstock Images
Interior Photos: Shutterstock Images, 1, 6, 8, 16 (top), 17, 22, 26, 27 (bejgli), 27 (bibingka), 27 (stollen), 27 (pavlova), 27 (pan de pascua), 27 (Yorkshire pudding); iStockphoto, 5, 7, 9, 11, 12, 13, 14, 15, 16 (bottom), 17 (top), 19, 20, 23, 25, 28, 29, 30; Cindy Hopkins/ Alamy, 21, 31

Editor: Connor Stratton
Series Designer: Jake Slavik

Content Consultant: Kristy Nabhan-Warren, PhD, Professor of Religious Studies and Gender, Women's and Sexuality Studies, University of Iowa

Library of Congress Control Number: 2019954994

Publisher's Cataloging-in-Publication Data

Names: Hamby, Rachel, author.

Title: Christmas / by Rachel Hamby.

Description: Minneapolis, Minnesota : POP!, 2021 | Series: Cultural celebrations | Includes online resources and index.

Identifiers: ISBN 9781532167676 (lib. bdg.) | ISBN 9781532168772 (ebook)

Subjects: LCSH: Christmas--Juvenile literature. | Holidays-- Juvenile literature. | Social customs—Juvenile literature

Classification: DDC 394.2663--dc23

WELCOME TO DiscoverRoo!

Pop open this book and you'll find QR codes loaded with information, so you can learn even more!

Scan this code* and others like it while you read, or visit the website below to make this book pop!

popbooksonline.com/christmas

*Scanning QR codes requires a web-enabled smart device with a QR code reader app and a camera.

TABLE OF
CONTENTS

CHAPTER 1
A WINTER HOLIDAY

Waking up on Christmas is exciting for

many people. Gifts wait under the tree.

Stuffed stockings hang from the fireplace.

Families and friends gather together.

It's a day of giving and receiving.

WATCH A
VIDEO HERE!

Giving gifts is a way people show love for one another on Christmas.

Christmas comes from the phrase "Christ's mass." During a traditional mass, Christians celebrate and remember Jesus.

Christmas began as a **religious** holiday. At Christmas, Christians celebrate the birth of Jesus Christ.

They believe he was the son of God.

Today, Christians and non-Christians both celebrate the holiday.

Families often prepare big meals and eat together.

Christmas Day is on December 25.
Some people start preparing in
November, and celebrations can run into
January. This stretch of time is called the
Christmas season. Many **cultures** around
the world have their own **traditions**
during it.

*Making and sending
cards is a common
way to celebrate.*

The Christmas season in Ethiopia includes several celebrations. Timkat is one of them.

DID YOU KNOW? People in Ethiopia follow a different calendar. So they celebrate Christmas on January 7.

CHAPTER 2
HISTORY OF CHRISTMAS

For thousands of years, people have celebrated the **winter solstice**. In the northern half of the world, this day occurs in late December. Ancient Romans held celebrations around this time of the year.

LEARN MORE HERE!

Many Christmas traditions, such as lights and wreaths, are based on winter solstice celebrations.

They sang songs and feasted. They also

decorated their homes.

Churches often use stained-glass windows to illustrate their teachings.

In the 300s, Christianity spread

throughout the Roman Empire. Church

leaders wanted Christians to celebrate

Jesus. But the Bible does not give the

date of his birth. So leaders chose

December 25. This date is close to the

winter solstice. As a result, many solstice

traditions became part of Christmas.

Bonfires are a key part of many winter solstice celebrations.

Over time, Christmas spread to new areas. People added new traditions. Christmas trees are one example. In the 1500s, Germans brought **evergreens**

Today, most Christmas trees have electric lights.

In early stories, Santa Claus filled stockings with toys.

into their homes. They decorated these

trees with candles. Another example is

Santa Claus. Dutch people started this

tradition in the United States.

DID YOU KNOW? Giving gifts to children on Christmas became popular during the 1800s.

CHRISTMAS TIMELINE

700s
Christmas celebrations spread to Scandinavia. The local symbol of a goat becomes part of the area's Christmas traditions.

336
The first known Christmas celebration takes place in Rome.

1500s
Germans decorate Christmas trees in their homes.

1700s
Dutch immigrants start the Santa Claus tradition in the United States.

1800s
Giving gifts to children becomes a part of Christmas. The day becomes more about families.

CHAPTER 3
RELIGIOUS TRADITIONS

For Christians, Christmas remains a **religious** holiday. Four Sundays before Christmas, Advent begins. The word *Advent* means "the coming of Christ." During this time, Christians remember the birth of Jesus. They often place candles around a **wreath**. Each Sunday, people

light one candle. These candles are

symbols of hope, love, joy, and peace.

A fifth candle goes in the middle of the Advent wreath. It is often lit on Christmas.

LEARN MORE HERE!

People often light candles during church services on Christmas Eve.

Many Christians attend church services too. They pray and sing songs. Many of the songs are about Christmas.

These songs are known as carols.

Christians also read from the Bible.

They listen to the story of Jesus's birth.

Christmas carolers often travel and sing holiday songs.

People in Mexico often eat Three Kings Bread, or Rosca de Reyes, on Epiphany.

Some Christians celebrate Epiphany

as well. This day happens on January 6.

The word *epiphany* means "to show or

reveal." On this day, many people believe

wise men came to visit Jesus. The wise

men revealed Jesus was the son of God.

On Epiphany, the city of Barcelona, Spain, hosts a parade. People dress up like the wise men.

DID YOU KNOW? The song "The 12 Days of Christmas" refers to the 12 days between Christmas and Epiphany.

CHAPTER 4
CULTURAL TRADITIONS

Many Christmas **traditions** are **cultural**.

They are not based on **religious** beliefs.

For example, baking cookies is a cultural

tradition. People also string lights around

COMPLETE AN ACTIVITY HERE!

The ornaments on a Christmas tree often represent people's memories or cultures.

Christmas trees. Many people hang a

plant known as mistletoe too.

Some traditions are specific to certain parts of the world. In the Philippines, for example, paróls light up the night. These colorful lanterns are shaped like stars. They are **symbols** of hope and belief.

The star shapes in paróls are symbols of the stars that guided the wise men to find the baby Jesus Christ.

DID YOU KNOW? In Argentina, Christmas comes in the summer. People decorate trees with cotton balls to look like snow.

CHRISTMAS TREATS

People around the world often bake traditional desserts for Christmas.

Bejgli (Hungary)

Bibingka (Philippines)

Stollen (Germany)

Pavlova (New Zealand and Australia)

Pan de Pascua (Chile)

Yorkshire Pudding (United Kingdom)

People often wrap gifts in red or green, the colors of Christmas.

Giving gifts is another cultural tradition. Many people buy presents for loved ones. Families tend to open gifts on Christmas morning. Some put gifts inside stockings. However, some people do not buy presents. For them, Christmas is a time to help others or be with the people they love.

SANTA CLAUS

Some traditions mix religion and culture. For example, Santa Claus comes from Saint Nicholas. He was the Christian saint of children. In the United States, people often show Santa wearing a red suit and white beard. In many stories, Santa gives gifts to children on Christmas Eve. He flies from house to house in a sleigh.

MAKING CONNECTIONS

TEXT-TO-SELF

Do you celebrate Christmas? Why or why not?

TEXT-TO-TEXT

Have you read books about other holidays
that people celebrate? What do they have
in common with Christmas? How are
they different?

TEXT-TO-WORLD

Countries around the world have different
Christmas traditions. Why might this be
the case?

GLOSSARY

culture – the ideas, lifestyle, and traditions of a group of people.

evergreen – a plant or tree that tends to stay green all year.

religious – having to do with a set of beliefs.

symbol – something that stands for something else because of certain similarities.

tradition – a belief or way of doing things that is passed down from person to person over time.

winter solstice – the day with the longest night of the year.

wreath – festive greenery put in a circle shape.

INDEX

ONLINE RESOURCES
popbooksonline.com

Scan this code* and others like it while you read, or visit the website below to make this book pop!

popbooksonline.com/christmas

*Scanning QR codes requires a web-enabled smart device with a QR code reader app and a camera.